FLYING CREATURES

Paper Airplane Book

69 Mini Planes to Fold and Fly

Ken Blackburn and Jeff Lammers

Workman Publishing, New York

To my wife, Lauren—my best friend and partner in every aspect of life.
Paper airplanes are the icing on the delicious cake of life she baked.   —KB

To the spirit of aviation—paper airplanes are where everyone starts.   —JL

Copyright © 2017 by Ken Blackburn and Jeff Lammers
Cover background © 2017 TTstudio/fotolia

Library of Congress Cataloging-in-Publication Data is available.

ISBN 978-0-7611-9380-7

Design by Jean-Marc Troadec
Cover and interior photos by Walter Chrynwski
Plane graphics: Saurian, Eagle, Dragon, Vampire, and Scarab by Shi Chen;
Stingray and Spectator by Jeffrey Pelo; Beach Bomber by Robert Zimmerman; Serpent by Garth Glazier;
Stinger by Janice McDonnell; Predator by Paul Woods; Beetlebot by Brad Hamann.

Workman books are available at special discounts when purchased in bulk for premiums and sales promotions
as well as for fund-raising or educational use. Special editions or book excerpts can also be created to specification.
For details, contact the Special Sales Director at the address below, or send an email to specialmarkets@workman.com.

Workman Publishing Co., Inc.
225 Varick Street
New York, NY 10014-4381
workman.com

WORKMAN is a registered trademark of Workman Publishing Co., Inc.

Printed in China
First printing August 2017

10 9 8 7 6 5 4 3

CONTENTS

Welcome to the World of Miniature Aviation

IN MOST WAYS, mini paper airplanes are much like full-size paper planes. They fly for the same reasons and are adjusted in the same way, but little planes do have some special characteristics. They are more agile than their bigger counterparts—they turn faster and are more sensitive to adjustments. Their smaller size also gives them the appearance of being very fast (even though they actually fly at the same speed as bigger paper planes). Mini planes are ideal for indoor flying—in part because there's no wind to buffet them about or to carry them off, and also because they're so tiny, it's easy to lose them outdoors.

BEST-BET FOLDING TIPS

All the pocket flyers are marked with dashed and dotted lines. The dashed lines are what we call "fold-in" lines, which means that they will be on the inside of a crease; you won't be able to see them once you make the fold. They are numbered in the order you should make the folds.

The dotted lines are "fold-away" lines. You'll be able to see them on the outside of the crease; they act as guides to help you know that you're folding in the right place. Some planes require cutting; cut lines are indicated by thick solid lines.

Try to make your creases as sharp as possible. It's wise to run a fingernail over the edge after you make a fold. This will especially help with the planes that have a lot of folds in one area, like the Spectator.

ADJUSTING THE PLANES

Even if you've folded your plane exactly as indicated, there's a good chance that it won't fly well at first. Almost all paper airplanes need a little fine-tuning. Bear in mind that with small paper airplanes, even tiny adjustments can have extreme results. For example, if a little "up elevator" is required for a level glide, adding only a small amount more may cause the plane to loop.

The first thing to check is that the wings are even and form a slight "Y" shape with the body. (In aviation speak, this is called dihedral.)

DIHEDRAL

Most planes fly best if the wings form a slight "Y" shape with the body.

UP AND DOWN

Adjusting the elevator is probably the next most important fix—it can keep your plane from stalling (slowing, then swooping to the ground and crashing) or diving. The elevator on a paper airplane is usually located at the back edges of the wings. If your plane is diving, add a little up elevator by bending the back edges of the wings up a little. If it's stalling, you may have added too much up elevator. Flatten the back edges of the wings.

ELEVATOR

Adjust elevator up or down at the back edges of the wings.

LEFT AND RIGHT

Most paper airplanes have a tendency to turn when they are first thrown. This can be fixed by adjusting the rudder of the plane. On most paper airplanes, the rudder is the back of the body (fuselage). To adjust it, bend it a little to the right or left. If your plane isn't flying straight, bend the rudder in the direction you want it to go. For example, if your plane is veering off to the right, bend the rudder a little to the left, and vice versa. If your plane flies straight and you want it to turn right, bend the rudder to the right. Do the opposite for the left.

SENDING THEM SOARING

A good flight requires a good throw. For most planes, your best bet is to pinch the body (fuselage) toward the front, using your thumb and index finger. Hold the plane level just in front of your shoulder and toss it forward. (The Serpent, Stinger, and Eagle use different throws; they're described in the folding instructions for those planes.)

LOOPS AND DIVES

The Spectator, Vampire, and Scarab are all good planes for stunt flying.

To do loops, add a lot of up elevator to your plane—much more than you usually would. Hold your plane a little behind your shoulder and give it a gentle toss straight up. Your plane should climb a few feet, stop, flip over backward, dive at the ground, then pull up before hitting the floor.

You also need a lot of up elevator for dives. Hold your planes as high above your head as you can and a little in front of you. Point the nose straight down and drop the plane. It should swoop down and pull out of the dive before it hits the floor.

EXPERIMENT!

Each model in this book is unique. Experimentation is the quickest way to learn how a plane flies best. Test-fly your planes, trying different adjustments and faster and slower throws. Generally speaking, the larger and wider the wings, the slower an airplane can successfully fly and the better it will glide. Airplanes with smaller wings usually fly faster and are better suited for long distances. But don't accept our word on this; fold up some planes and find out for yourself!

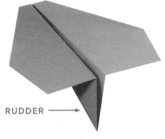

RUDDER →

Bend the rudder in the direction you want your plane to go.

SAURIAN

MYTHOLOGY IS FILLED with legends of ferocious flying dragons. Now you can conjure up one of your own faster than any wizard. The Saurian is easy to build and is a graceful flyer. It also has better breath and is less likely to set fire to the curtains than a real dragon!

FLYING TIPS

The Saurian flies best with the back of the tail angled up a little so the tips of the tail are above the wing. Make sure the head is straight (if it is bent to one side, the plane will begin to turn). Slipping a paperclip over the Saurian's nose will help ensure a smooth flight.

Making the Saurian

Cut on solid lines; fold in on dashed lines (so they are no longer visible); fold away on dotted lines.

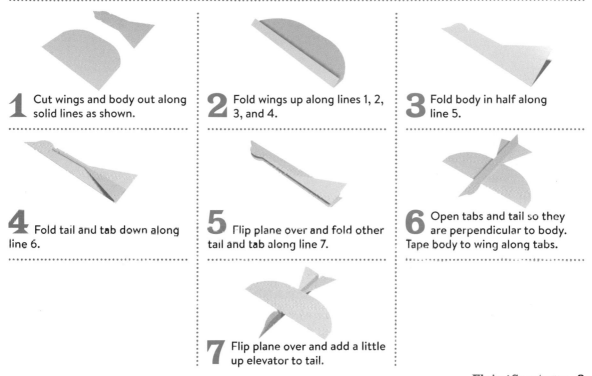

1 Cut wings and body out along solid lines as shown.

2 Fold wings up along lines 1, 2, 3, and 4.

3 Fold body in half along line 5.

4 Fold tail and tab down along line 6.

5 Flip plane over and fold other tail and tab along line 7.

6 Open tabs and tail so they are perpendicular to body. Tape body to wing along tabs.

7 Flip plane over and add a little up elevator to tail.

STINGRAY

IF YOU WATCH a stingray swim, it almost looks as though it's flying through the water. These ocean creatures have "wings" of up to 5 feet across. Your Stingray is a great flyer, too, but it does much better in the air than the sea. It's good for both straight long-distance flights and graceful circles around the room.

FLYING TIPS

For best flying, use a little up elevator on the back edge of the fuselage. Launch by gently holding outside edges and tossing forward. For right turns, bend the back of the left wingtip down and the back of the right wingtip up. Reverse this for left turns.

Making the Stingray

Fold in on dashed lines (so they are no longer visible); fold away on dotted lines.

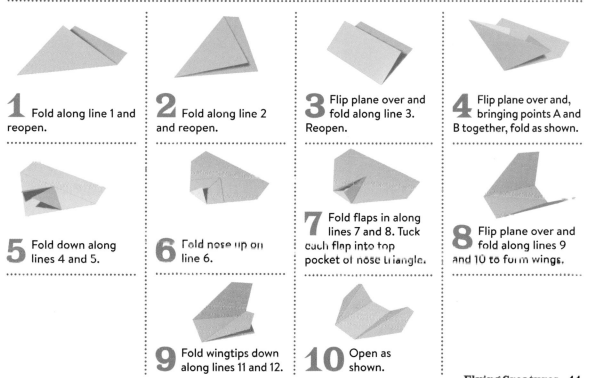

1 Fold along line 1 and reopen.

2 Fold along line 2 and reopen.

3 Flip plane over and fold along line 3. Reopen.

4 Flip plane over and, bringing points A and B together, fold as shown.

5 Fold down along lines 4 and 5.

6 Fold nose up on line 6.

7 Fold flaps in along lines 7 and 8. Tuck each flap into top pocket of nose triangle.

8 Flip plane over and fold along lines 9 and 10 to form wings.

9 Fold wingtips down along lines 11 and 12.

10 Open as shown.

SPECTATOR

WE ALL NEED an extra set of eyes. Send a pair on a reconnaissance mission around your home. The Spectator is a resilient plane; it's great for flights across the room but is equally agile outside. It's also suitable for doing loops and dives.

FLYING TIPS

For the best flights, the plane should form a slight "Y" shape when viewed from the front. If it nosedives, add some up elevator. Bend the rudder to the right for right turns or left for left turns.

Making the Spectator

Cut on solid lines; fold in on dashed lines (so they are no longer visible); fold away on dotted lines.

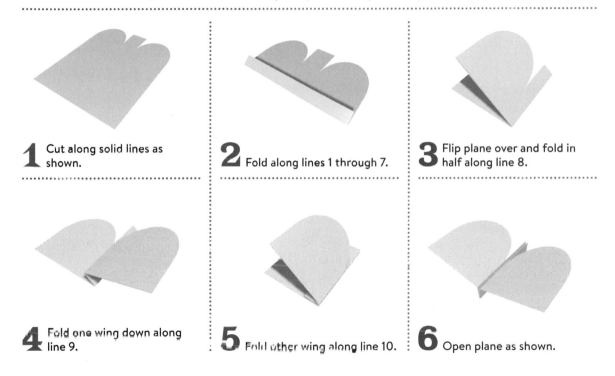

1 Cut along solid lines as shown.

2 Fold along lines 1 through 7.

3 Flip plane over and fold in half along line 8.

4 Fold one wing down along line 9.

5 Fold other wing along line 10.

6 Open plane as shown.

BEACH BOMBER

DON'T BE SCARED by this giant radioactive fly. It may look like it's ready to attack, but it's actually just considering whose picnic to land on next. The Beach Bomber is a stable, smooth flier best suited for calm-air soaring.

FLYING TIPS | This plane should form a slight "Y" shape when viewed from the front. If the plane dives, add a little up elevator. To make it turn, bend the back of the vertical tails in the direction you want to go.

Making the Beach Bomber

Cut on solid lines; fold in on dashed lines (so they are no longer visible); fold away on dotted lines.

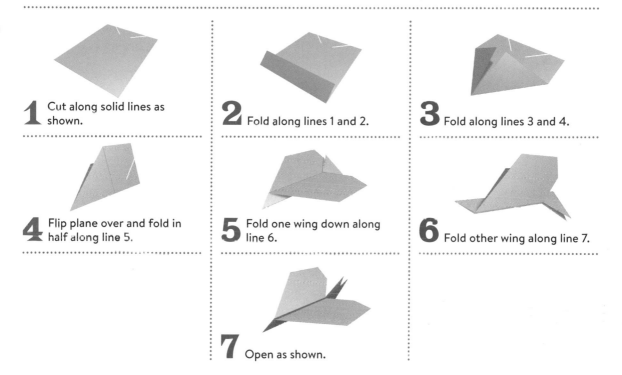

1 Cut along solid lines as shown.

2 Fold along lines 1 and 2.

3 Fold along lines 3 and 4.

4 Flip plane over and fold in half along line 5.

5 Fold one wing down along line 6.

6 Fold other wing along line 7.

7 Open as shown.

SERPENT

THERE ARE MORE than 3,000 types of snakes, but this is the only one that can really fly. The "flying" snake of Southeast Asia actually just jumps from the tops of trees. The Serpent is great at gliding silently through your house, and it is a sturdy outdoor flyer, too.

FLYING TIPS | To launch, pinch the front of the plane with your index finger on the top and thumb on the bottom. Hold in front of your eyes with the front of the plane forward, gently pull the plane away from you, and release. Bend both points on the back edges of the wings up for the best flight.

Making the Serpent

Fold in on dashed lines (so they are no longer visible); fold away on dotted lines.

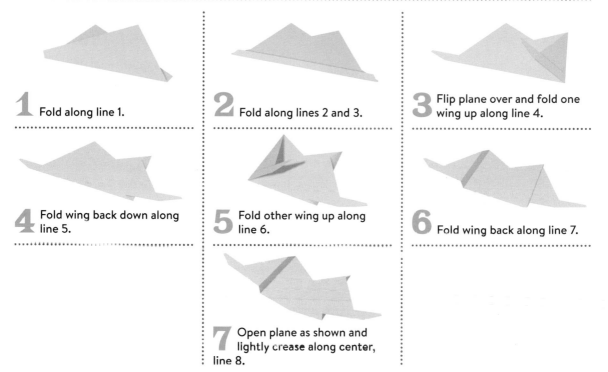

1 Fold along line 1.

2 Fold along lines 2 and 3.

3 Flip plane over and fold one wing up along line 4.

4 Fold wing back down along line 5.

5 Fold other wing up along line 6.

6 Fold wing back along line 7.

7 Open plane as shown and lightly crease along center, line 8.

STINGER

THE STINGER'S LONG, narrow wings make it a great glider. This plane is reminiscent of the high-performance sailplanes made by the Horton Brothers of Germany in the 1930s. Although it flies smoothly indoors, on a calm day it really shines outdoors. Try a gentle toss from a hill for a spectacular flight!

FLYING TIPS

Launch this plane in the same way as the Serpent (see page 16). It needs a lot of up elevator—bend up the back edges of the wings a little. To correct unwanted turns, use more up elevator on the wing opposite the direction the plane is turning.

Making the Stinger

Cut on solid lines; fold in on dashed lines (so they are no longer visible); fold away on dotted lines.

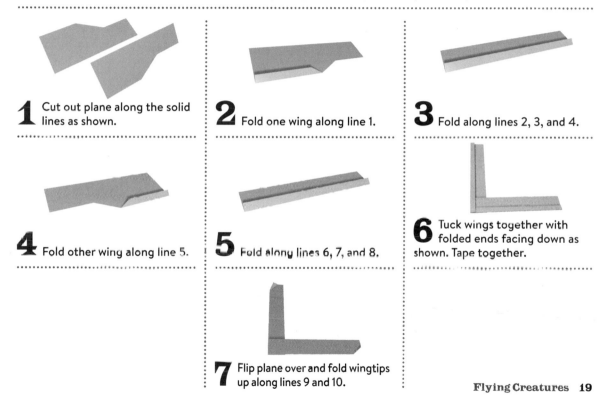

1 Cut out plane along the solid lines as shown.

2 Fold one wing along line 1.

3 Fold along lines 2, 3, and 4.

4 Fold other wing along line 5.

5 Fold along lines 6, 7, and 8.

6 Tuck wings together with folded ends facing down as shown. Tape together.

7 Flip plane over and fold wingtips up along lines 9 and 10.

PREDATOR

THIS JET IS as at home in the salty depths as it is in the sky. Jet power and the ocean may not seem to go together, but there actually have been several jet-powered sea planes, including the supersonic Convair F2Y Sea Dart. This plane excels at long, accurate indoor flights.

FLYING TIPS

Bend up the back edge of each wing. Make sure the wings are either level or gently angled upward to form a slight "Y" shape when viewed from the front, and that both "engines" are straight, not skewed left or right.

Making the Predator

Cut on solid lines; fold in on dashed lines (so they are no longer visible); fold away on dotted lines.

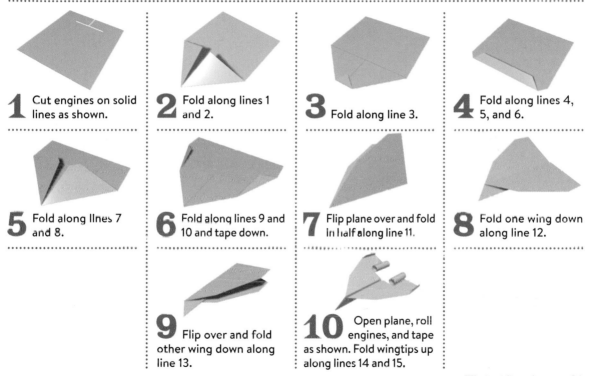

1 Cut engines on solid lines as shown.

2 Fold along lines 1 and 2.

3 Fold along line 3.

4 Fold along lines 4, 5, and 6.

5 Fold along lines 7 and 8.

6 Fold along lines 9 and 10 and tape down.

7 Flip plane over and fold in half along line 11.

8 Fold one wing down along line 12.

9 Flip over and fold other wing down along line 13.

10 Open plane, roll engines, and tape as shown. Fold wingtips up along lines 14 and 15.

EAGLE

MANY PEOPLE WONDER how this aircraft flies, considering it has no wings. In fact, it works something like a biplane. The top of the cylinder acts like the upper wing and the bottom acts like the lower wing. Be prepared to draw a crowd—people are amazed it flies at all.

THROWING TIP

To throw the Eagle, slip the wide side of the aircraft (between the two points is good) between your pointer and the rest of your fingers, with the folded edge facing out. Flick your hand and arm forward. The Eagle flies best with the points on the back edge bent upward a bit.

Making the Eagle

Fold in on dashed lines (so they are no longer visible); fold away on dotted lines.

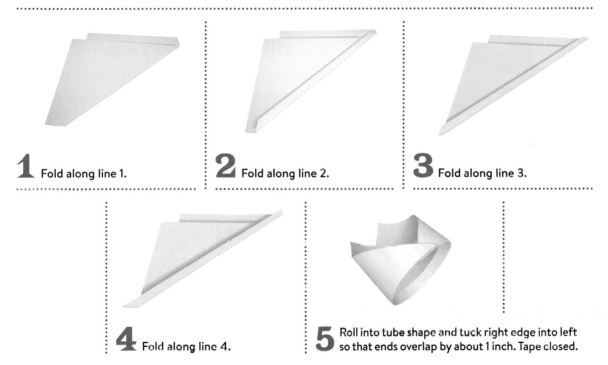

1 Fold along line 1.

2 Fold along line 2.

3 Fold along line 3.

4 Fold along line 4.

5 Roll into tube shape and tuck right edge into left so that ends overlap by about 1 inch. Tape closed.

DRAGON

THIS PLANE WAS inspired by the supersonic jet the Concorde, which from 1976 till 2003 carried passengers across the Atlantic at more than twice the speed of sound. Your model may be a bit slower, but it's a good glider for both distance and accuracy.

FLYING TIPS | Make sure the wings are symmetrical and form a slight "Y" shape with the body. Bend the back edges of wings up for slower, longer flight. Leave wings flat to get closer to supersonic speeds.

Making the Dragon

Cut on solid line; fold in on dashed lines (so they are no longer visible); fold away on dotted lines.

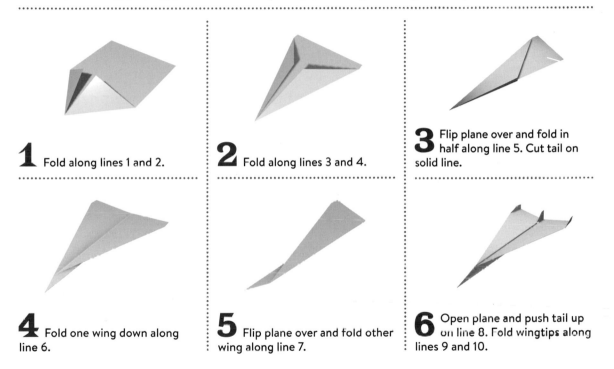

1 Fold along lines 1 and 2.

2 Fold along lines 3 and 4.

3 Flip plane over and fold in half along line 5. Cut tail on solid line.

4 Fold one wing down along line 6.

5 Flip plane over and fold other wing along line 7.

6 Open plane and push tail up on line 8. Fold wingtips along lines 9 and 10.

BEETLEBOTS

YOU WON'T FIND these among the million species of insects in the world, but they are great flyers nonetheless. See if you can get your Beetlebots to turn a corner so that you can "bug" someone in the next room.

FLYING TIPS | Make sure the center of the wings are level and the outboard wings (outside of folds 7 and 8) are angled upward. Also bend the pointed part of the back of each wing up a little.

Making the Beetlebots

Cut on solid line; fold in on dashed lines (so they are no longer visible); fold away on dotted lines.

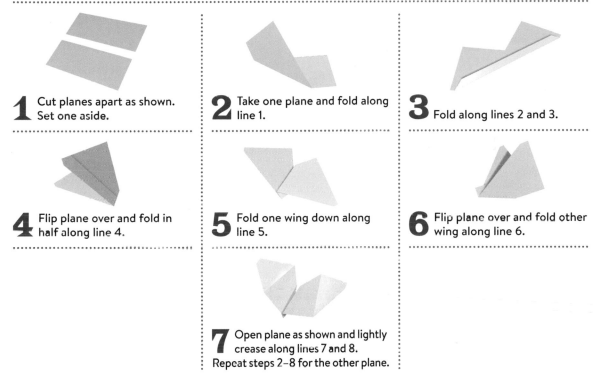

1 Cut planes apart as shown. Set one aside.

2 Take one plane and fold along line 1.

3 Fold along lines 2 and 3.

4 Flip plane over and fold in half along line 4.

5 Fold one wing down along line 5.

6 Flip plane over and fold other wing along line 6.

7 Open plane as shown and lightly crease along lines 7 and 8. Repeat steps 2–8 for the other plane.

VAMPIRE

THE TWIN TAIL booms and straight wing of this model were inspired by the British fighter the de Havilland Vampire, which was one of the first jets to be introduced after World War II. Your Vampire is a great flyer and can even be adjusted to do loops and dives.

FLYING TIPS

For normal flight, use a little up elevator. For loops, use a lot of up elevator and gently throw the plane straight up. For dives, use a lot of up elevator and release the plane from high over your head with the nose pointing down.

Making the Vampire

Cut on solid lines; fold in on dashed lines (so they are no longer visible); fold away on dotted lines.

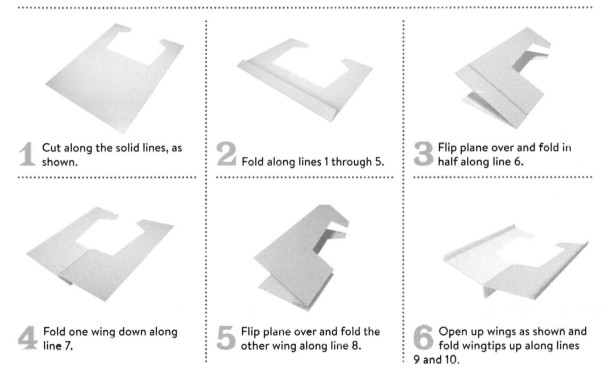

1 Cut along the solid lines, as shown.

2 Fold along lines 1 through 5.

3 Flip plane over and fold in half along line 6.

4 Fold one wing down along line 7.

5 Flip plane over and fold the other wing along line 8.

6 Open up wings as shown and fold wingtips up along lines 9 and 10.

SCARAB

NO NEED TO call the exterminator. This is one beetle you'll enjoy flying around the house. It doesn't buzz, crawl, sting, or tickle you with its antennae. Instead, it glides quietly around the room. If you want, it will perform turns and even loops.

FLYING TIPS | The Scarab may need a little down elevator for general flying and up elevator for doing loops or turns. Make sure that the points on the front of the plane are straight before flying.

Making the Scarab

Fold in on dashed lines (so they are no longer visible); fold away on dotted lines.

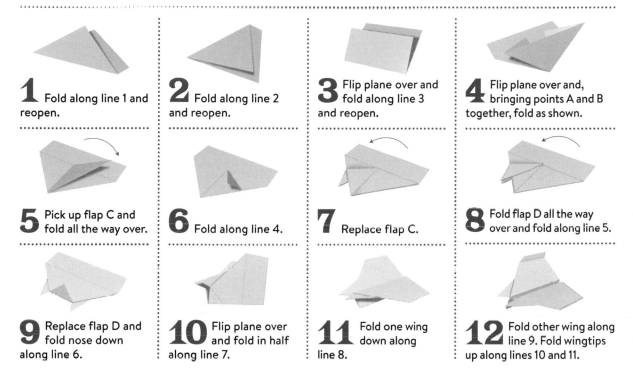

1 Fold along line 1 and reopen.

2 Fold along line 2 and reopen.

3 Flip plane over and fold along line 3 and reopen.

4 Flip plane over and, bringing points A and B together, fold as shown.

5 Pick up flap C and fold all the way over.

6 Fold along line 4.

7 Replace flap C.

8 Fold flap D all the way over and fold along line 5.

9 Replace flap D and fold nose down along line 6.

10 Flip plane over and fold in half along line 7.

11 Fold one wing down along line 8.

12 Fold other wing along line 9. Fold wingtips up along lines 10 and 11.

Flight Log

Date	Airplane Name	Longest Time Aloft	Greatest Distance Flown

The Flying Creatures Squadron

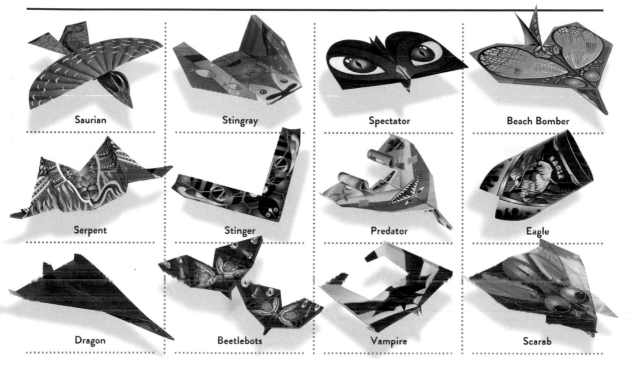

Saurian

Stingray

Spectator

Beach Bomber

Serpent

Stinger

Predator

Eagle

Dragon

Beetlebots

Vampire

Scarab

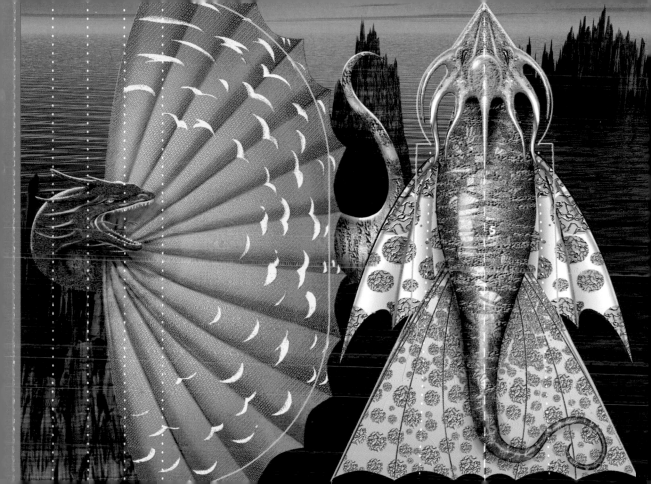

TAPE
BODY
HERE

7 9 4 3 2 1

TAPE
BODY
HERE

4   3   2   1

7   6

TAPE
BODY
HERE

TAPE BODY HERE

4 3 2 1

9

TAPE
BODY
HERE

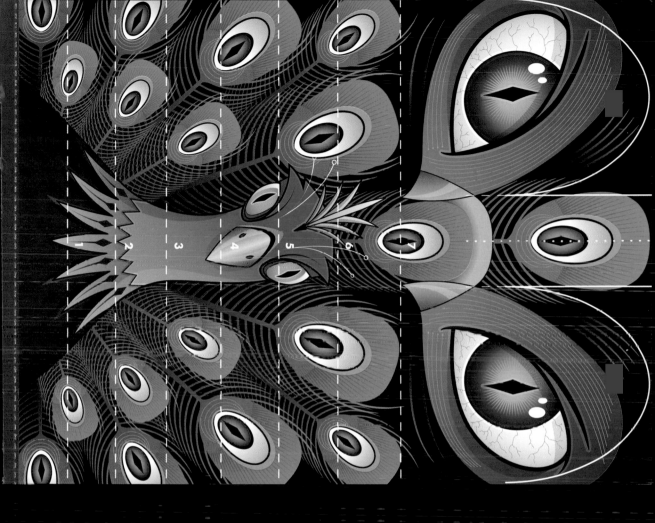

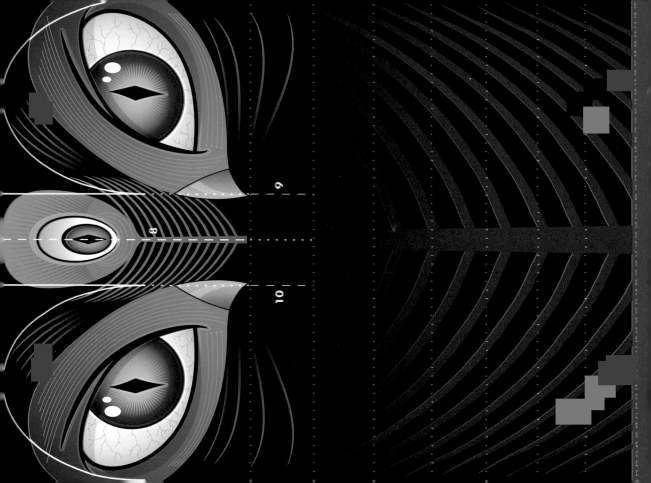

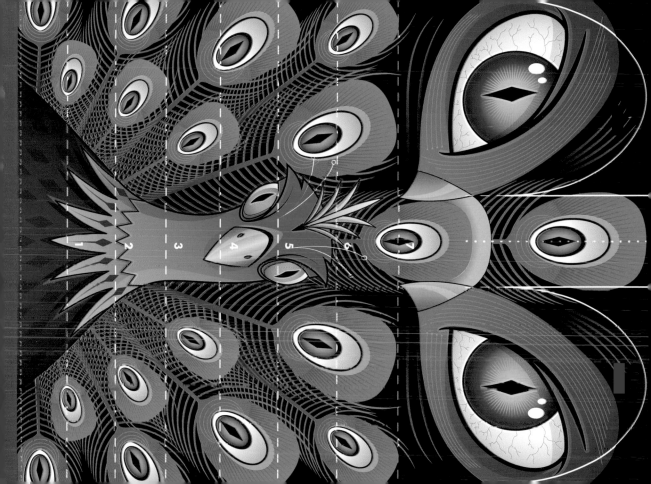

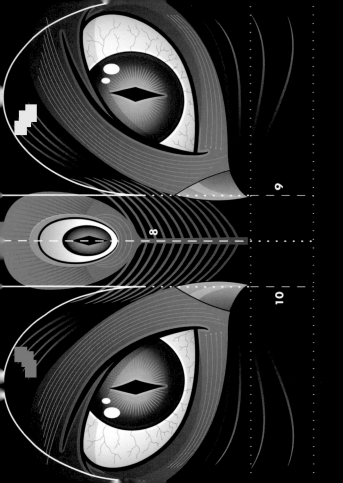

8

9

10

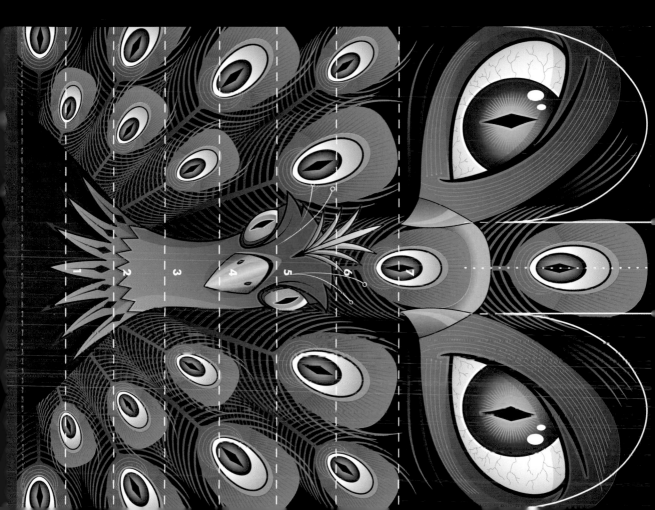

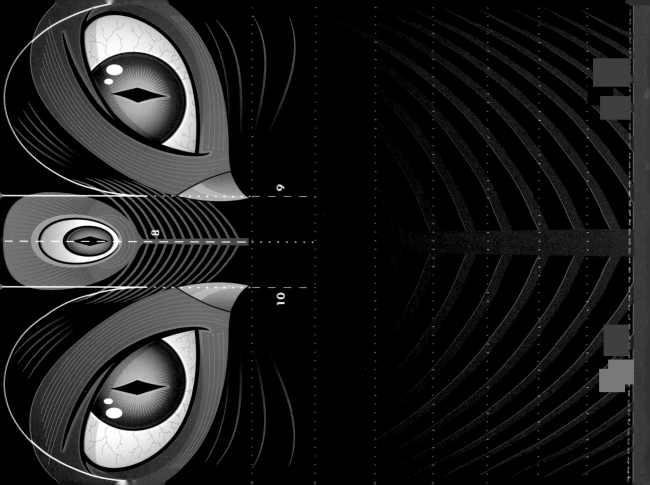

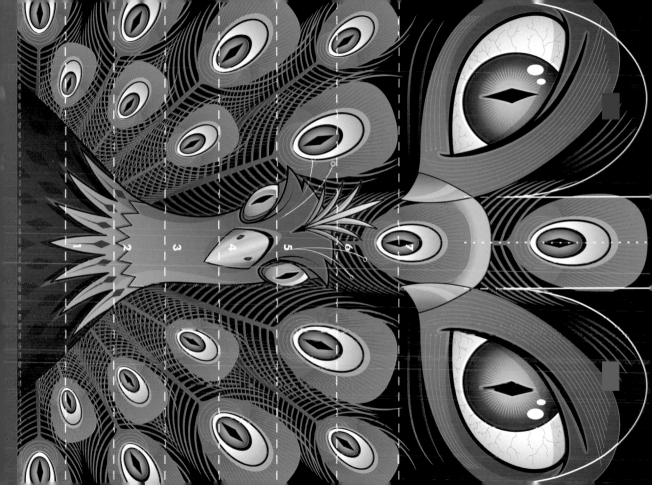

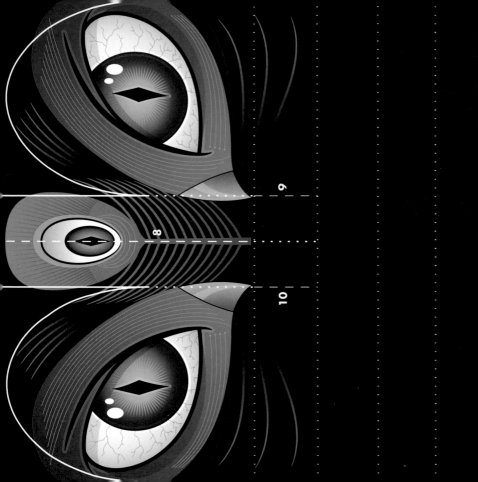

8

9

10

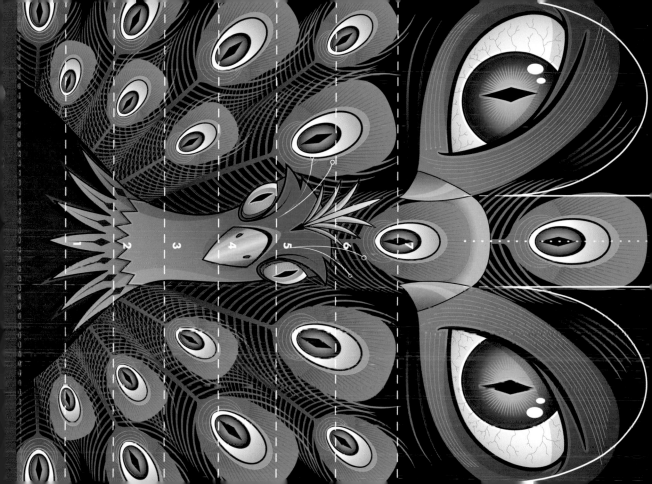

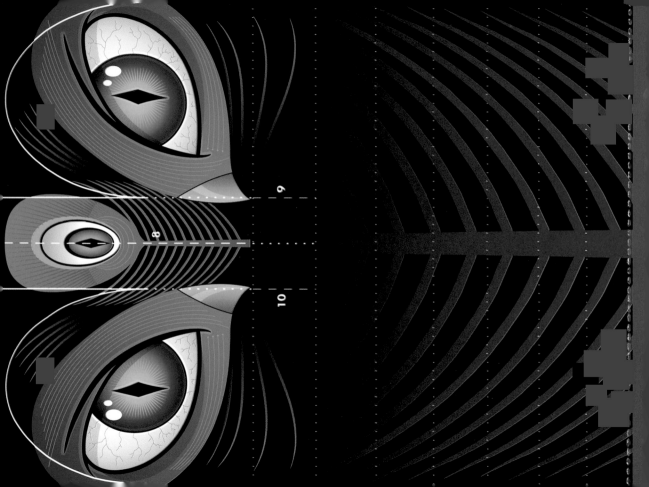

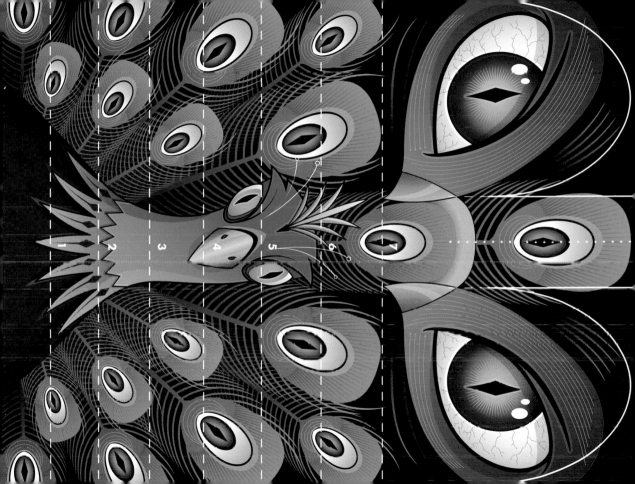

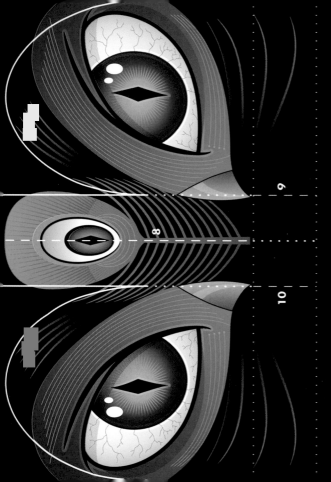

9

8

10

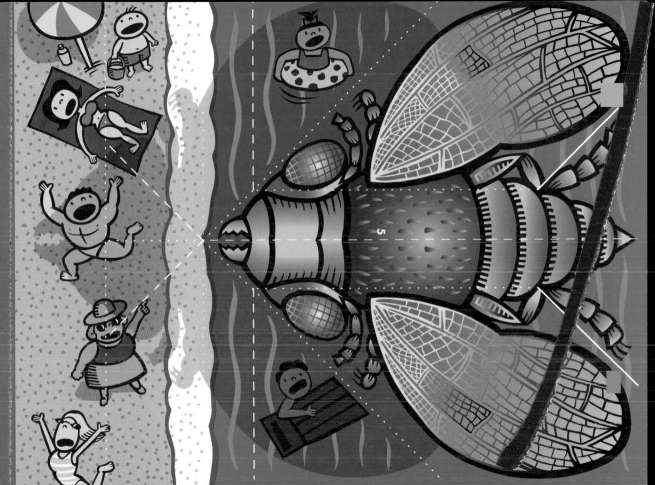

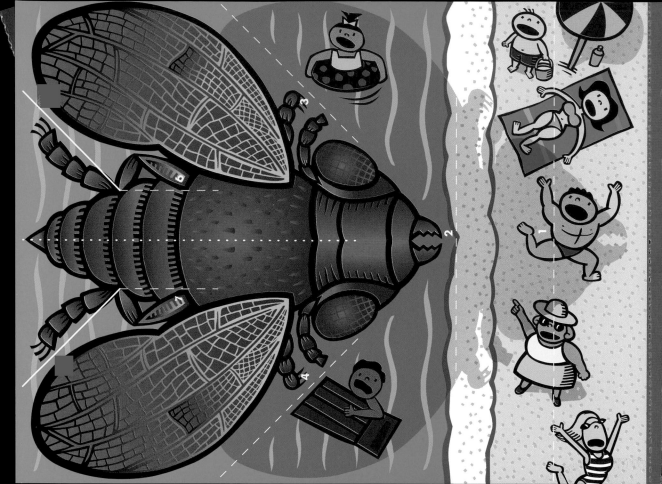

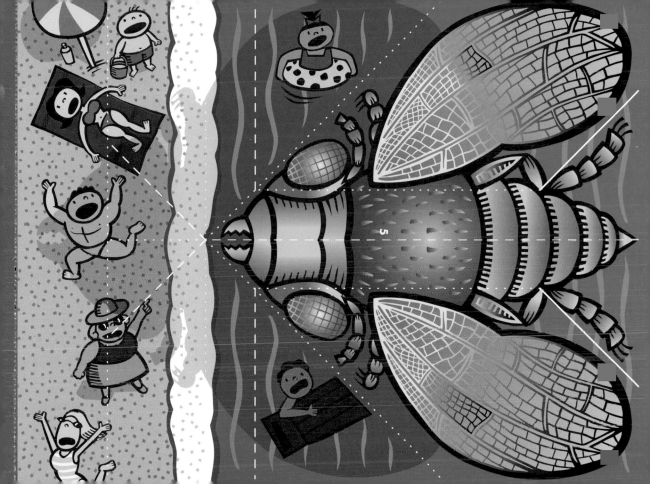

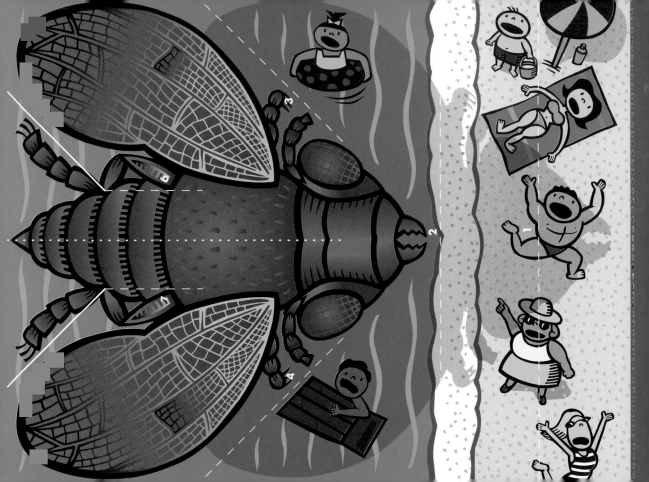

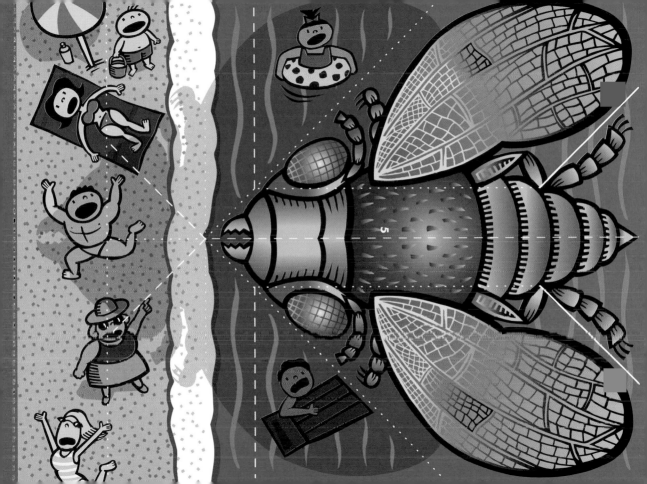

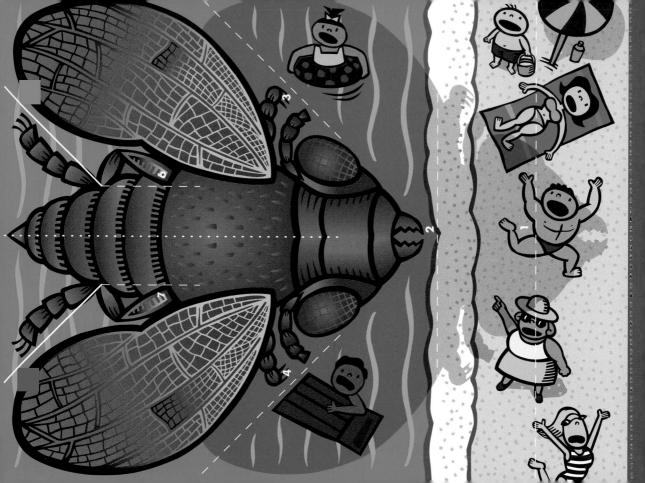

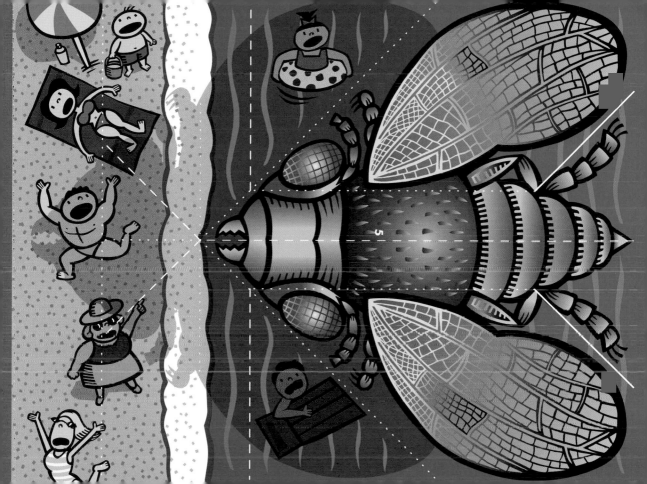

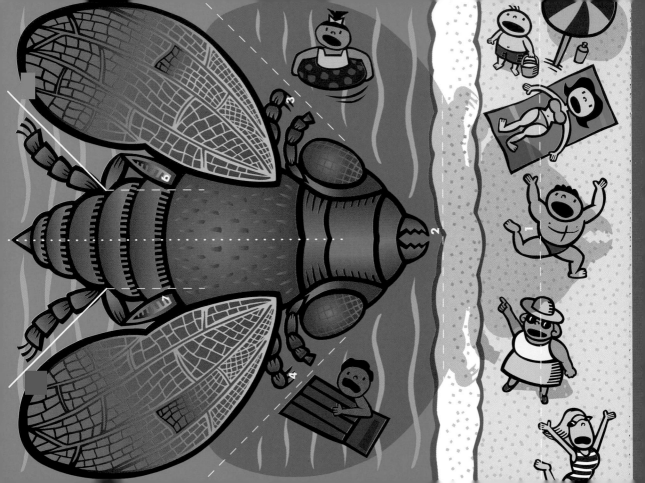

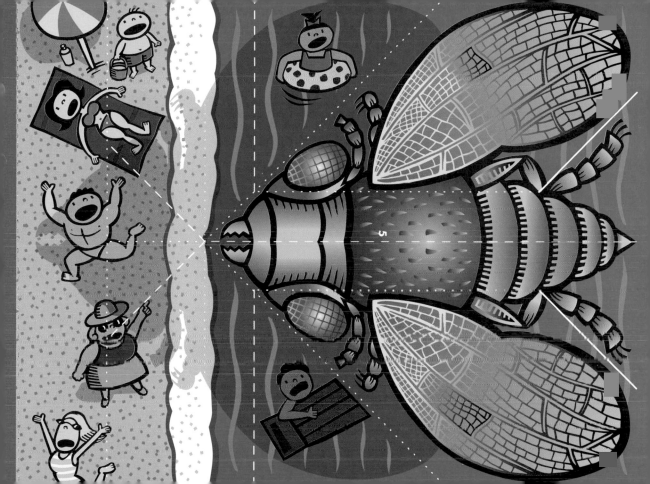

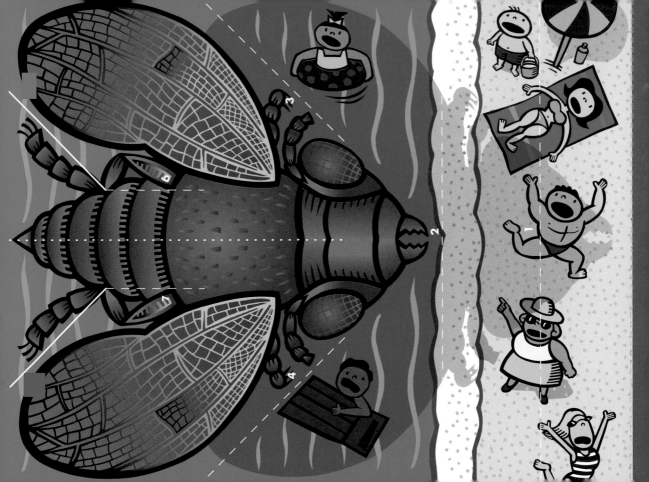

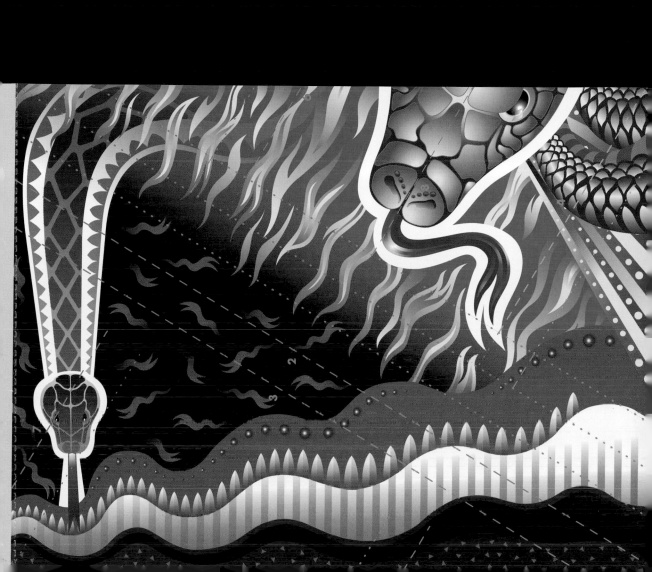

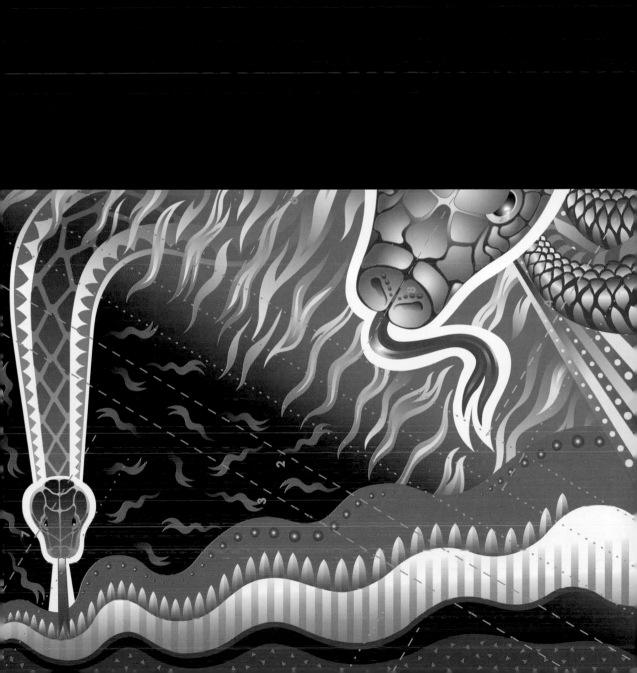

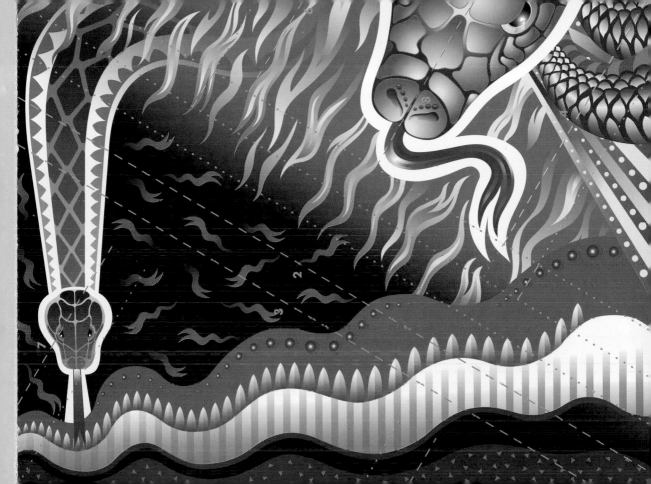

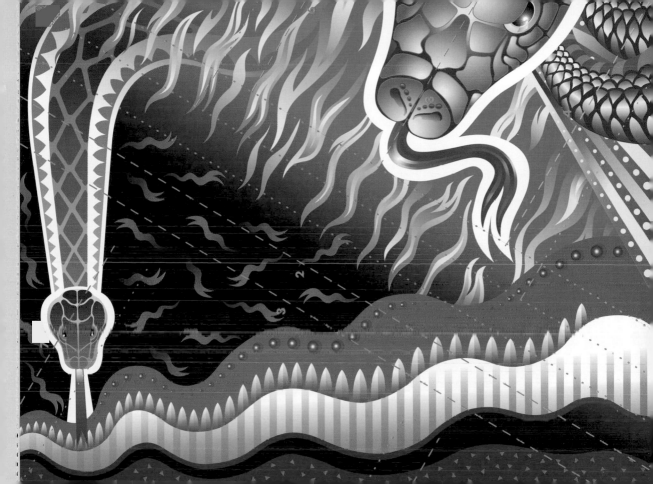

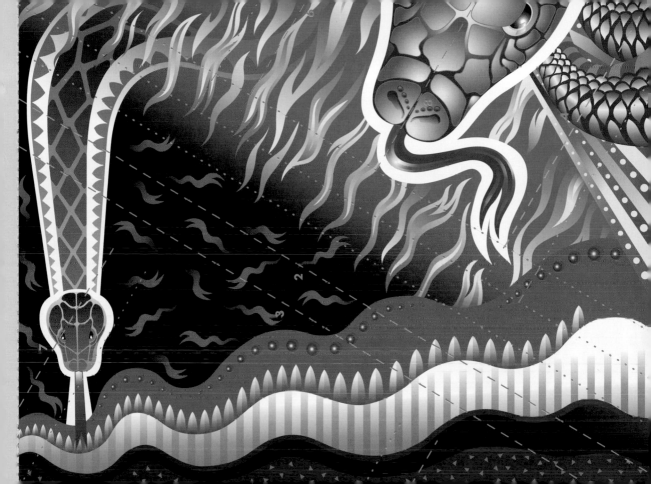

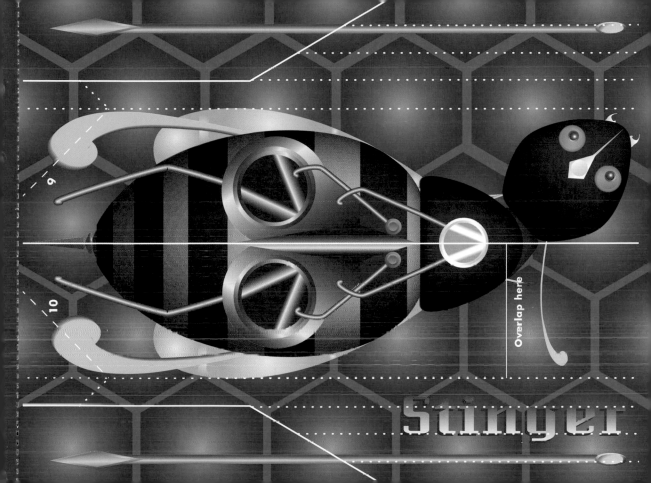

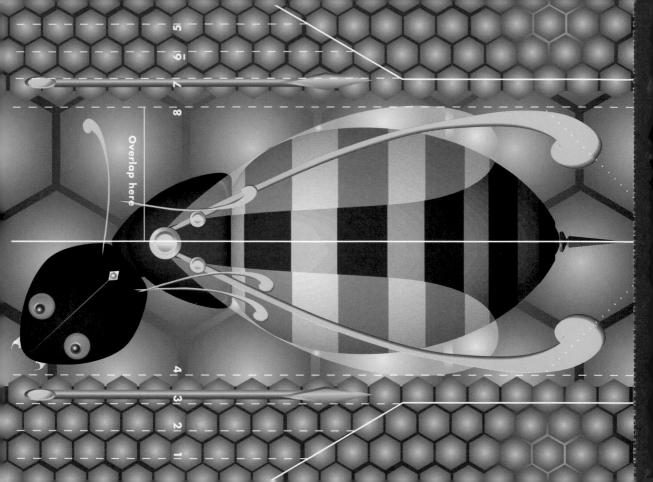

Overlap here

5
6
7
8

4
3
2
1

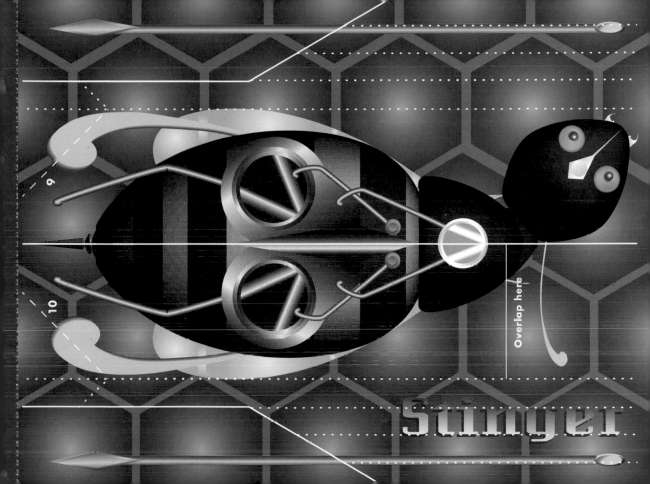

10

9

Overlap here

Stinger

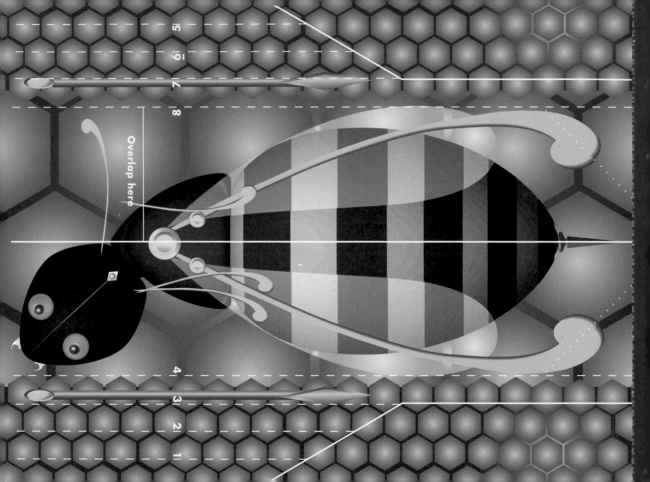

Overlap here

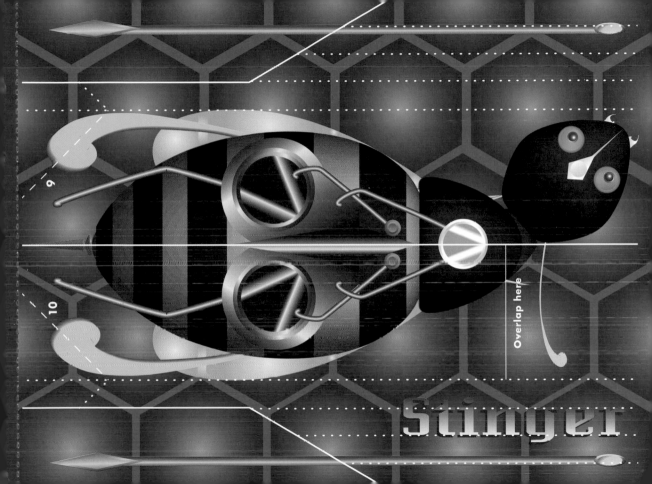

Overlap here

Stinger

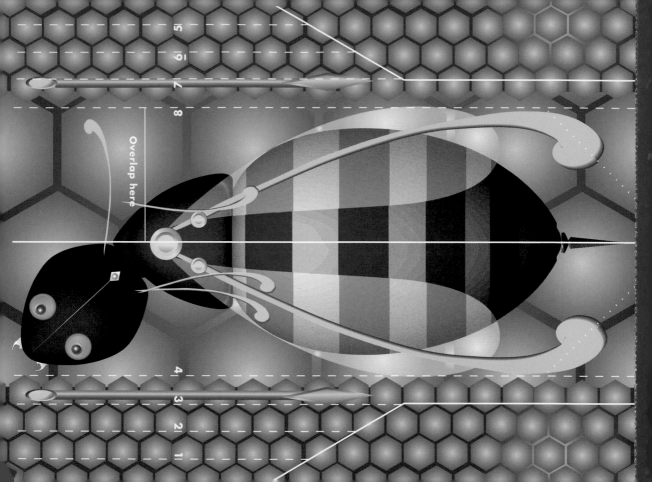

Overlap here

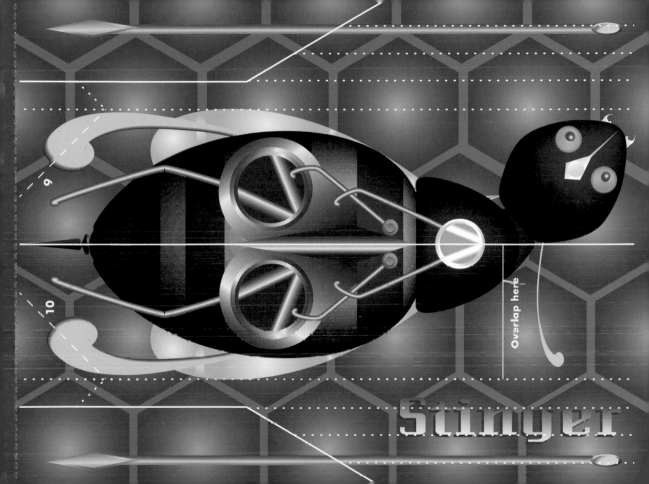

Overlap here

Stinger

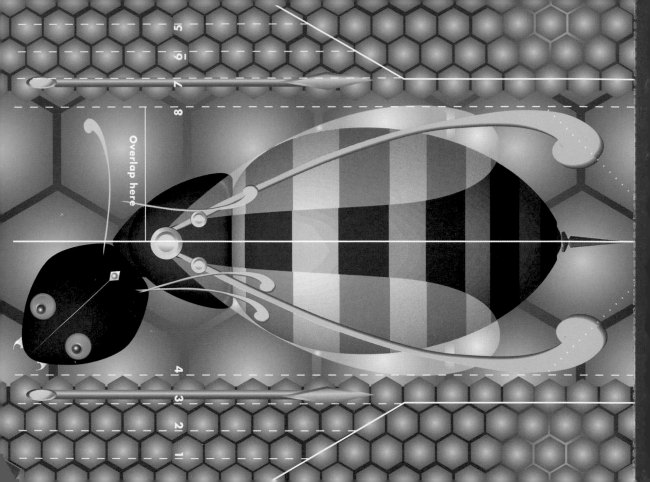

Overlap here

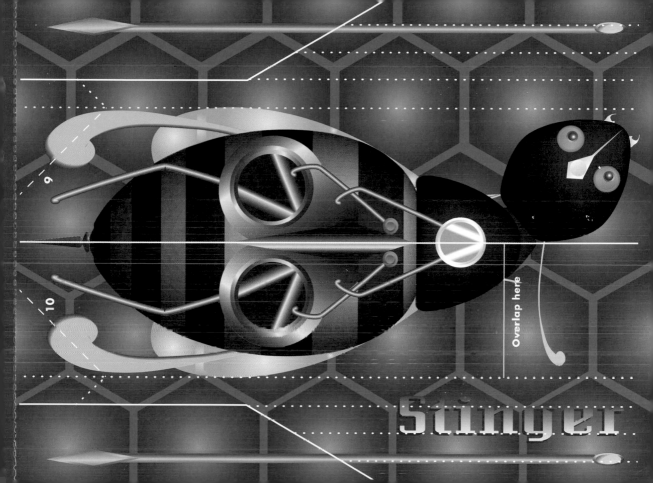

9

10

Overlap here

Stinger

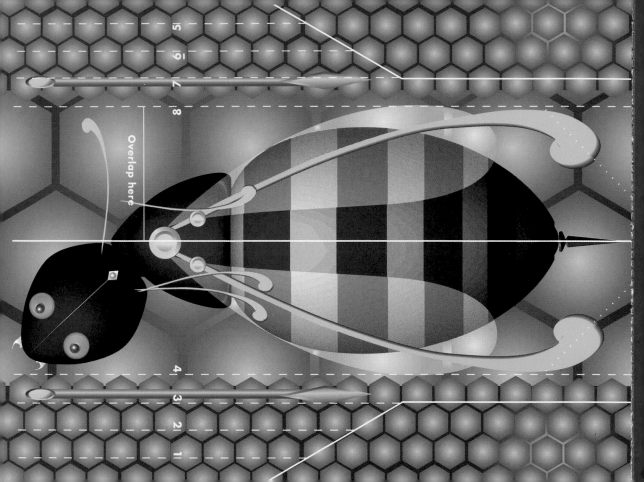

Overlap here

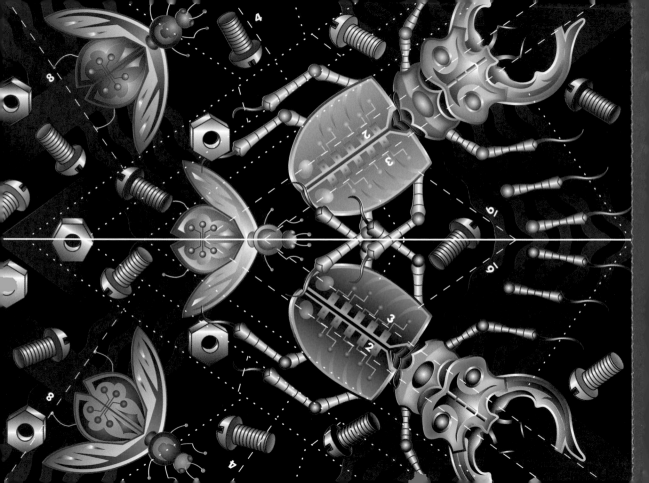

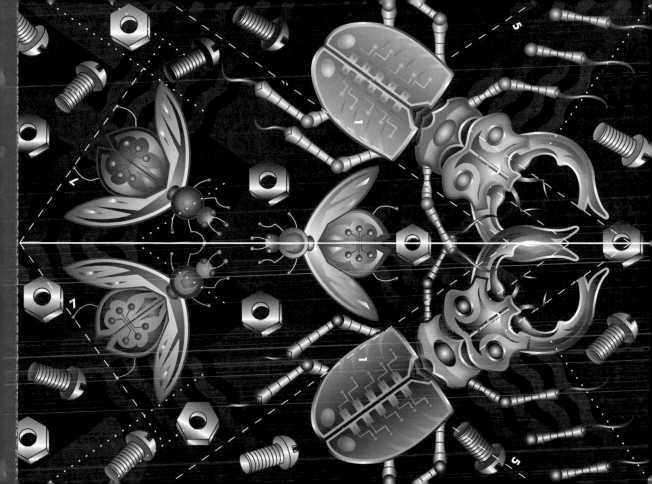

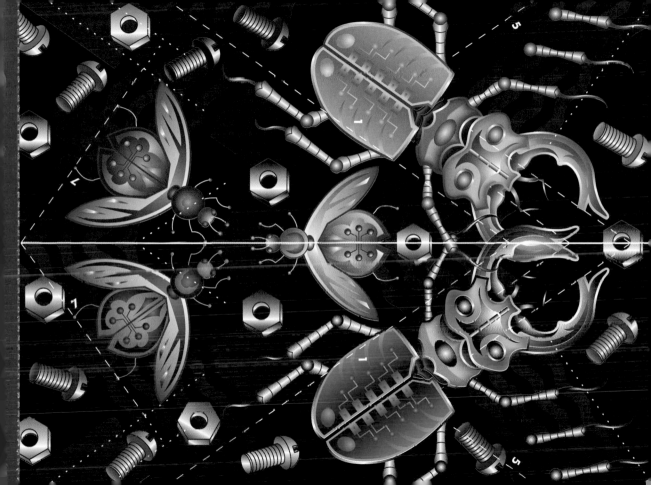

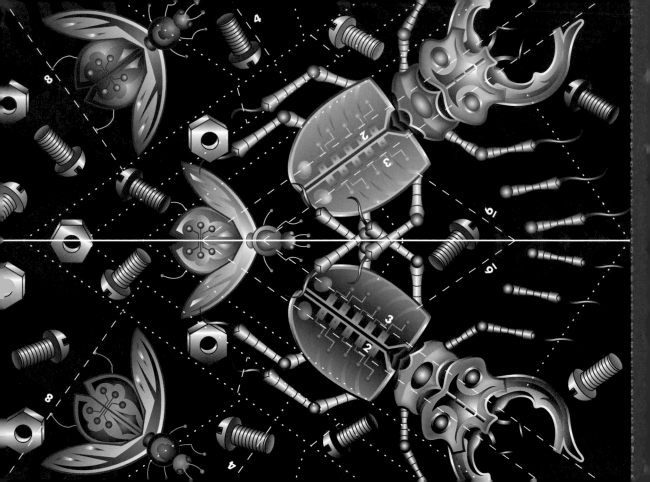

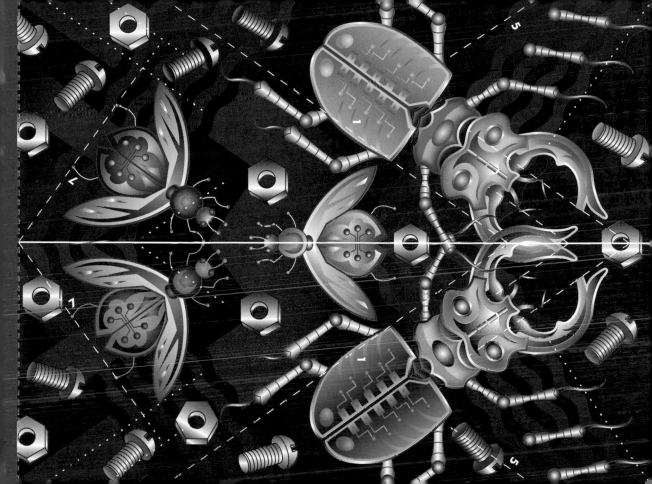

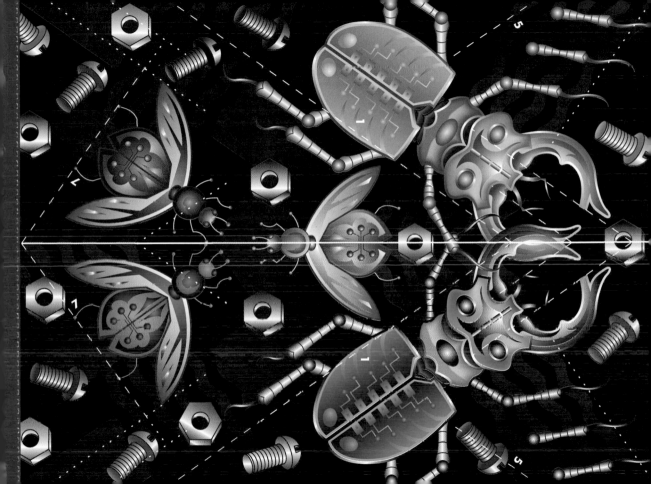

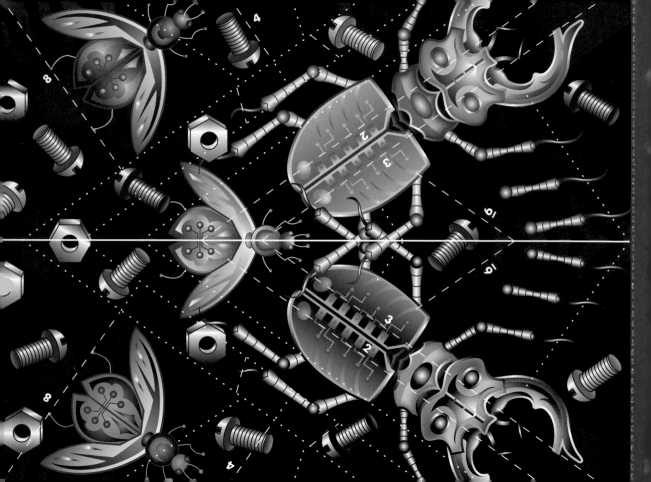

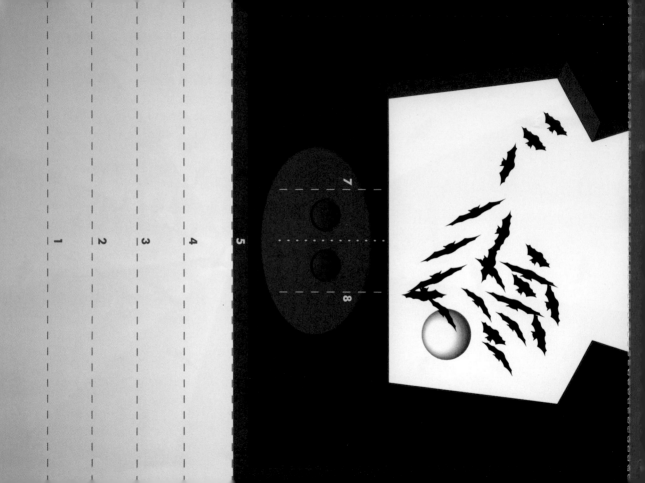

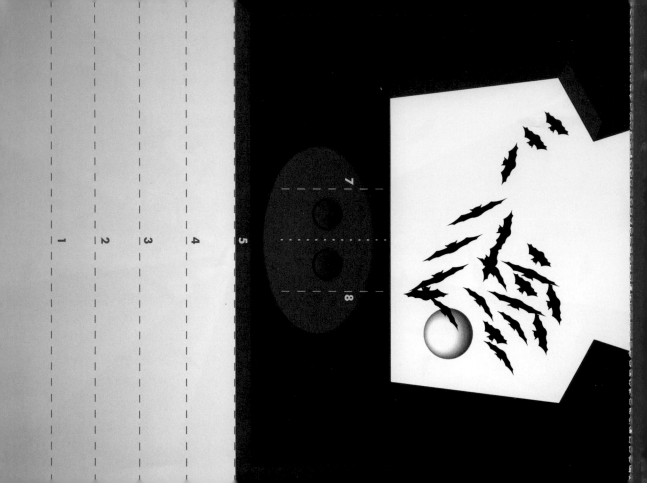

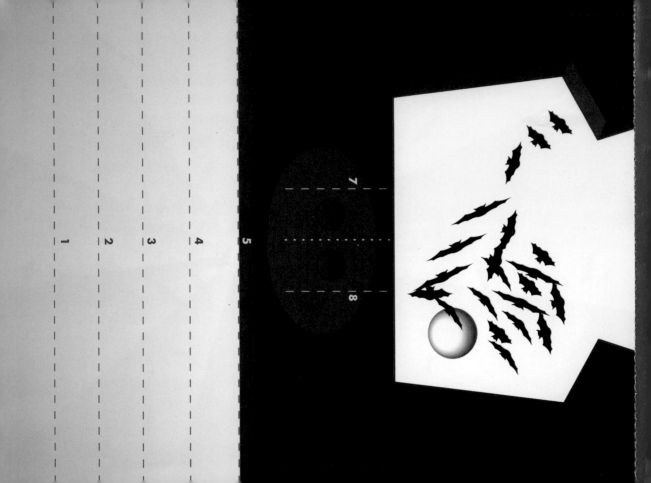

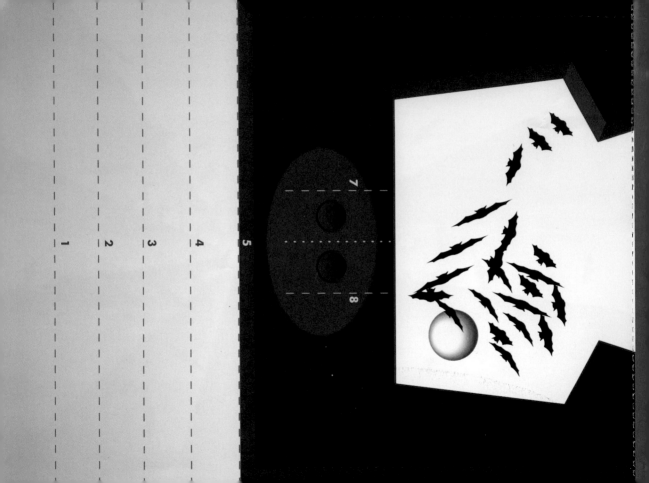

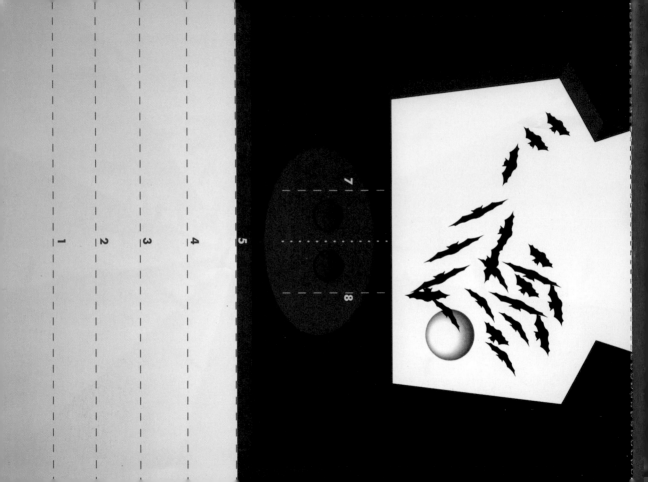

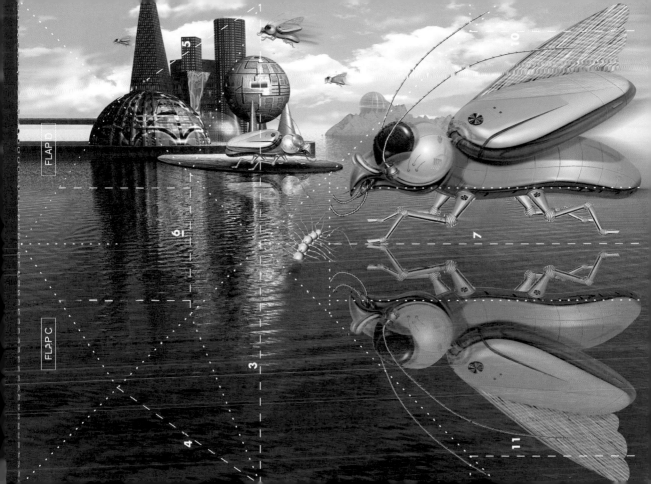

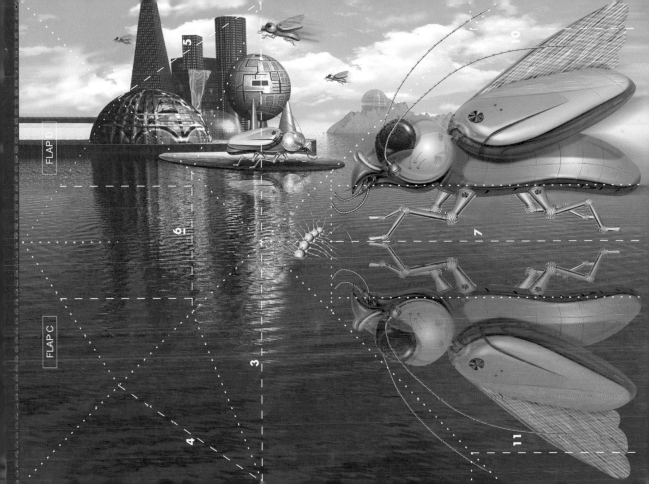

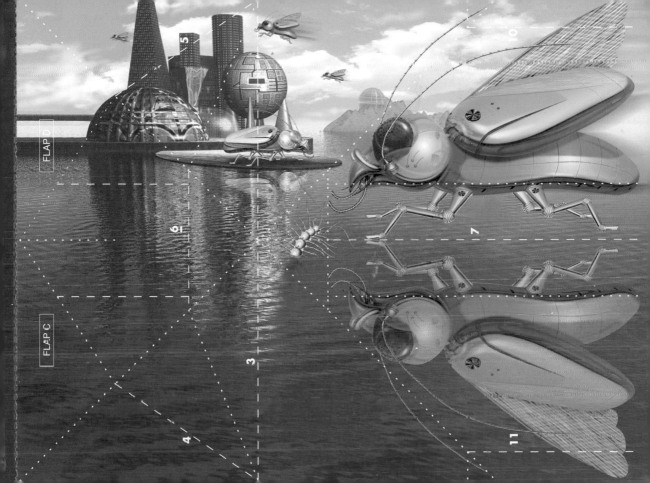